Bending the Arch

Bending the Arch

Poems

ROSE MARIE BERGER

Foreword by Dana Greene

RESOURCE *Publications* · Eugene, Oregon

BENDING THE ARCH
Poems

Resource Publications
An Imprint of Wipf and Stock Publishers
199 W. 8th Ave., Suite 3
Eugene, OR 97401

www.wipfandstock.com

PAPERBACK ISBN: 978-1-5326-6000-9
HARDCOVER ISBN: 978-1-5326-6001-6
EBOOK ISBN: 978-1-5326-6002-3

Manufactured in the U.S.A.   JANUARY 8, 2019

God builds and unbuilds Worlds; and who shall build up that Arch that was broke down at the Deluge?

Thomas Burnet, 1691

Contents

Permissions

Foreword

ONE ENTERS *BENDING THE ARCH* lured by sound and rhythm. A multitude of voices dislocates, doing what poetry can do: provoke. The long poem, "Confessions of a Westward Expansionist," uses an Ur language lifted up from peoples and cultures all speaking across time and place. It begins with the catenary curve of steel, architect Eero Saarinen's steel arch, built in Saint Louis, guardian of the mighty Mississippi, constructed as the gateway to the West, symbol of the conquering of land and people and the realization of America's "Manifest Destiny," that 19th-century belief that the expansion of the American government throughout the continents was justified, inevitable, and divinely ordained.

This is a poem of national history, of the meeting of America's acclaimed heroes with Ute and Paiute, Shoshone, Cheyenne, Pawnee, Pomo, and Chumash, with recently emancipated Africans, Irish immigrants, and Chinese rail workers. It is the saga of encountering frontiers of flooding rivers, drought-haunted earth, punishing mountains. The sins of the nation are all here in this westward colonization and domination. This becomes backdrop for the author's personal history and for our corporate heritage. It is this history which shapes us and is our legacy.

The question posed by this tangling together of history and evocative word is whether human creativity in the form of art—poetry and ritual especially—can redeem? "Confessions of a Westward Expansionist" gives no definitive answer. Rather it offers the juxtaposition of divergent languages and rituals—Hebrew, Spanish, French, liturgical Latin with Chumash, Pomo, Sioux—over against America's national transgressions. Saarinen's arch, that monument to national expansion from Europe and the East to the Pacific and the West, is a marker of triumph, aligned against this history of pain and marginalization. "Confessions" is a thundering, unrelenting, sardonic expression which exposes this history, and as such is reminiscent of the words of the biblical prophet Jeremiah: "'Is not my word like as a fire?' saith the Lord; 'and like a hammer that breaketh the rock in pieces?'" Perhaps our rock needs to be broken in pieces. Can prophetic art do this?

Here the history of America's grievous offences are met by a particular form of American spirituality, Catholic in its origin, incarnational in its implications. Here is hope in human artistic creativity. While art may not absolve us, it can provoke and awaken us as a nation and as persons. We are enmeshed in the American sin, the American brokenness; we inherit it. And it is our work to come alive to this reality and to redeem it, make it whole, to rescue us from the past which has made us who we are. *Bending the Arch* is an act of remembering the past for the sake of the future.

Dana Greene

Dana Greene is dean emerita of Oxford College of Emory University and author of biographies of Evelyn Underhill, Maisie Ward, Denise Levertov, and Elizabeth Jennings. She writes frequently for the National Catholic Reporter.

Preface

How do we enter the stories of others?

Sofia Samatar, author of *Tender*, offers a short catalogue. "There's missionary efforts . . . colonialism . . . or through the pursuit of knowledge, through the sciences, through commerce, through trade, through literature and language." The poems in this collection offer many of these entrances.

But Samatar makes another discovery. "It's not about trying to figure out how we enter the stories of others. We are *made* of the stories of others." Our received family stories naturally put us at the center. But when we decenter our own narrative enough to glance toward the edges we find strange questions: Who was the native family with the "pretty horses" that remained in my grandmother's memory for nine decades? What did my Irish Catholic great grandparents fleeing the Famine Roads think about the formation of "Indian reservations"—modeled on English colonialist attempts to drive native Irish beyond the River Shannon and off arable land? "See how deeply entangled you are with people you wouldn't necessarily consider your own," notes Samatar.

This approach is dangerous. When we who are settlers and colonialists (no matter what else we may be) entangle our stories with others, we are predisposed by culture and social systems to dominate and enslave the stories of "the other" to serve our own ends. The domination dynamic threatens in these poems also.

Ethnopoetic documentary poetry, such as in *Bending the Arch*, draws from verifiable fact and is informed by the unverifiable fact of imagination, as Muriel Rukeyser puts it. But when the "ethno" portion is framed through the settler lens—where politically, socially, and theologically dominion still rests—it must be interrogated to the point its power becomes either generative or set aside. That is the reader's responsibility.

I started "Confessions of a Westward Expansionist" in response to my own sense of cultural dislocation. I am a cultural Californian, a West Coaster, and Catholic who has lived for more than half my life in the culture of the Anglo-Protestant urban East and in neighborly relations with people who mostly migrated from the rural South to Washington, D.C. Since I migrated East from the Sacramento valley, I've been trying to get my footing, find my standing ground.

On a trip to St. Louis in the mid-1990s during one of the great spring floods, I dreamed that I was looking west through the Gateway Arch, designed by architect Eero Saarinen in 1947. Instead of seeing the Mississippi River, I saw the Pacific Ocean, two thousand miles away. In an instant, something ignited in me: I wanted to know about the spiritual powers in operation between St. Louis and the Pacific in the age of expansion and extermination, an age which my Irish Catholic and German Mennonite immigrant family took part only three generations ago.

Examining one's personal history reveals threads that tangle communities together. As a "practicing" Roman Catholic (I'll keep practicing until I get it right), I recognize a wellspring of wisdom in my tradition—a creation-saving, beauty-laden wisdom I don't want lost. The litanies of plant and animal life in *Bending the Arch* cultivate affection for our creaturely community, a community struggling to survive. And yet, the harm of the Church's "Christianizing, civilizing, enslaving" project, in particular the way the Doctrine of Discovery shapes a Christian-colonial worldview even today, will take at least 400 years to repair, heal, make whole. "It's not about entering," says Samatar, "it's about seeing where you are."

This collection is a cry for help. Our ancient stories and storytenders are all that will save us in this age of climate catastrophe. But spiritual imagination has atrophied in modernity and post-modernity. In *The Great Derangement*, Amitav Ghosh writes, "We have entered a time when the wild has become the norm: if certain literary forms are unable to negotiate these torrents, then they will have failed—and their failures will have to be counted as an aspect of the broader imaginative and cultural failure that lies at the heart of the climate crisis."

In this "catastrophozoic" era, poetry may have the imaginative muscles necessary to navigate the torrents, the new wild. Retracing our steps through 19th-century first encounters—when worlds were torn apart—is a quest for spiritual knowledge, a miraculous realism, equal to human-to-human encounters and human encounters with the nonhuman. Climate change will decolonize us, eventually. Our stories and the unverifiable facts of imagination might show us how to remake ourselves together.

For some readers, it may be helpful to skim through the notes at the back of the collection as a way of orienting to the encounter with language and voices.

Rose Marie Berger
Feast of St. Hildegard of Bingen
Washington, D.C.

Acknowledgments

To David Leslie Wimmer, my godson, for whom this poem began, and his mother, Carol Leslie. To Dennis Nurkse for not flinching in the face of my vision and coaching me through its birth. With gratitude to Monique Sonoquie (Chumash/Apache/Yaqui) for her permission to include the Santa Rosa Island Chumash language. To Marcia, Tonantzin, and Ilhuicamina Rincon-Gallardo for *familia*. To Charlotte Lange, tribal chairperson for the Mono Lake Kutzadika'a Paiute Indian Community in Lee Vining, Calif., who are still fighting for federal recognition. To Julie Tumamait-Stenslie, tribal chairperson of the Barbareño/Ventureño Band of Mission Indians (Chumash) for her extensive commitment to preserving and advancing Chumash culture and for the protection and repatriation of Native American ceremonial artifacts. With deepest appreciation for conversations with Dr. Gabrielle Tayac (Piscataway) about the sacred community that gathers for the Sun Dance celebration, varying perspectives and sensitivities held among Indigenous individuals and nations regarding the Sun Dance, warning about activating deadly cultural frames around "primitive savagery," probing my own understanding of the movement of the divine, incarnation, and Christian sacrifice, and extending an invitation and sharing a trust in the power of spiritual resistance movements. Dr. Tayac, niece of Piscataway Chief Billy Redwing Tayac, served as a historian at Smithsonian National Museum of the American Indian for 20 years. In 2018, she became director of legacy collections with The Spirit Aligned Leadership Program. To Wendy DeGroat, for her exquisite ear and work in the area of documentary poetry. To the community of Jesus-followers at Sojourners. To my parents, Barbara Ely Bird Berger and John Henry Berger, and my Nebraska and Oregon family for memories of the homestead in Riverton (population in 1890 was 389, in 2010 it was 89) in the bottomlands of the Republican River and "seven hills from Red Cloud." To Joseph

Michael Berger (Gage, Sorelle, and Zev) and Catherine Ellen Berger Auble (and Howard). To Elaine Enns for deep thoughts on "mapping bloodlines, landlines, and songlines" as a practice of historical healing and transformative justice. To Ched Myers, theological animator and spirit friend, for his ministry of *paraklesis* (advocacy, accompaniment, and strengthening of heart). To the four-legged, finned, and winged *anam cara* and to Heidi Lyn Thompson, my beloved.

Prophecies from the Watershed Confederacy

In those days, when *the crown*
o'er the earth melted and humans
were thick upon the land

a sigh rose up and weeping
from rocks, rivers, hills:

abandon your house,
abandon what you possess,
build a boat instead.

Bless your *curach* with pine boughs
and singing. Kiss the runnels and rills,
estuaries and arroyos who bear you up.

Be born again
into water and living spirit.

*

Then from the heavens
sky-brothers fought;
the stars in their orbits did battle.

Moon and water rose as one,
rode roughshod over culvert,
subaltern sewer, corrugated pipe.

Pretty petals of the rich fell
slick, opaque against the muddy bank.
The stream Kishon swept

those lordly enemies away;
that ancient river, Kishon.

And Hashem kept his word to the fish.

To sleek, trinitarian salmon
who out-braved the Lords of profit,
Hashem said, 'Swim swiftly now.

Come hide in my headwaters
where the brothers will give you
strength, where against your enemies

the mothers will make ceremony,
even if they die, as the Maidu
warrior-women died defending

the River of Sorrows.'

And so they ran   up ladders, fords,
ledges, dams. From pool to resting pool,
flashing, slashing tails, lithe and pinked

with power, a fish-rush headlong
up the ancient river, cold as
silver, flecked and cut with broken

stars. Empty-stomached Chum, Chinook,
Coho, blessed with hunger for Hashem
and the Maidu-mother songs.

*

2

To the human remnant Hashem said:
'If you cannot see the water,
you will not see the Water Walker.

If you misconceive bread,
you will not conceive water.
Seek life instead of riches.'

Confessions of a Westward Expansionist

She takes cedar incense—cedar mixed with pine sap and sage—and sprinkles it on a fire before spreading the sweet smoke with an eagle feather. "It's a prayer to beg pardon for things being disturbed."

I. CAHOKIA

Never read this poem
in summer
when serpent god
dozes on the southern horizon—
one starry eye keeping watch
over hero and hawk

Read this poem
in pumpkin season
when corn can listen
and our Mother can rise

from her basket of bones
defend us under moonlight
bury her hatchet in serpent's side

This is how we are born

We are Cahokia: Tenochtitlan of the north

Our cities are peace:

Monk's Mound, Emerald Acropolis
Our faith breaks bows, blunts arrows

We made the American Middle Ages

While Rome hurled crusaders
at a holy land, we took our own
measure

> *Earth and myself are of one mind*
> *The measure of land*
> *and measure of our bodies*
> *are the same*

Twenty thousand strong
for four hundred years

Maize, our only gold

At Mound City our gates stood open

Before you conquer us again
look first on our mighty works

Only ceremony
can season us now
only earth take our measure

II. FOUR ANGELS

Thou shalt sprinkle me with hyssop
and I shall be cleansed

Four hundred more years
And across the river
another city
guided by other stars

Between Fourth and Broadway
in downtown Saint Louis
stands the old courthouse

It is framed
from one perspective
in Saarinen's inverted catenary curve
            the arch
that perfect monument to westward expansion
a view to space, an arrangement of intervals
in Thomas Jefferson's panopticon

> *Confidential: Gentlemen of the Senate*
> *Regarding Exploration of the West 1803*
>
> *Indian tribes residing within the limits of the United States*
> *have for a considerable time been growing more and more uneasy*
> *at the constant diminution of the territory they occupy*
> *and the policy has long been gaining strength with them*
> *of refusing absolutely all further sale of land to us on any condition*

In April's emerging light, the arch
—seen from the east across the Mississippi
now crested six-to-ten feet above flood stage
—casts off sun dogs and copper bows

In the old courthouse
also in April with warblers

and the rivers running high

Dred Scott

his
Dred X *of color*
name

and Harriett Robinson

his
X
wife

petitioned the court
for freedom

> *Because good rain knows its seasons*
> *born in spring it follows the wind*
> *comes secretly at night*

On the X where Dred is buried
a centennial plaque

> *Dred Scott*
> *Born about 1799*
> *Dred Scott subject of the decision, 1857*
> *Died September 17, 1858*
> *Dred Scott*

Three hundred and twenty years earlier
Portuguese caravels rode low
in the Gulf of Mexico

licking the maw of this Great River
their holds full of Negroes

> *Dred Scott object of decision, 1857*
> *by Supreme Court of the United States*
> *denied citizenship to any Negro*
> *void the Missouri Compromise*
> *one step closer to war*

Harriett
Dred
their daughters Lizzy and Eliza
first won freedom in a lower court

But Chief Justice Roger B. Taney
of a higher court
overturned the rule

> *A slave is not property in the sense*
> *that a lifeless thing is property*
> *but as cattle are property*
>
> *He has roughly the same kind*
> *of freedom as an animal*
> *which is allowed to graze*
> *and on occasion*
> *to beget or bear its young*

Here on Broadway in Saint Louis
William Clark died

> *Soldier explorer statesman and patriot*
> *His life is written in the history of his country*

(Virginian, slaveholder, Anglican, Indian agent

his life is written in the history of skin
and parchment maps)

on September 1, 1838
in the home of his son,
named for that other hero
Meriwether Lewis

Corps of discovery, those two
creatures of commerce

And York (dead of cholera in Tennessee
or resurrected and free
in the land of the Crow)

And Agaidika Sacajawea (enslaved
to Toussaint Charbonneau,
Catholic Quebecois) unsettles
the society of race, makes
bread to appear in wilderness

> *this bread I eat with great satisfaction* (Clark)
> *it being the only mouthful*
> *I had tasted for several months past*

Today the plane I'm in plunges
banks its wings
overshadows the brushed aluminum thighs
of Saarinen's majestic gateway

one foot on land, one foot on sea
a totality both intimate and brutal

Now I look down on
William Clark's granite obelisk
(all of Saint Louis mourned his passing)
It peaks through flood waters

covering Saint Louis
covering Bellefontaine Cemetery
covering the whole north side

Today
is Baptism Sunday

How did we get here?

On a Thursday, 1492,
Cristoforo Colombo
made first encounter
with Lukku-Cairi,
Tainos,
by handing them a sword
blade first.

Note, Colombo wrote,

> *They should be good servants and intelligent*
> *for I observed that they quickly took in*
> *what was said to them and I believe*
> *that they would be made easily into Christians*

Baptism Sunday
now nineteen hundred and ninety-three
the rivers Missouri and Mississippi
always generous
have overswept their banks

only the Mounds
west of Saint Louis
stare dry-eyed, prescient
into the sun

Watershed prophecies
from John the Revelator

The four angels bound
at the great rivers
have been released

III. FLOOD STAGE

For one hundred and forty-four days
Saarinen's arch
sank to its knees
in Mississippi mud and water

> *Roll Jordan roll*
> *Roll Jordan roll*

> *The saints cry*
> *The angels cry*

> *Everybody wanna go to heaven*
> *Nobody wanna to die*

In June, river levels in Mound City
twenty feet above flood stage
never been so high
not in a hundred and fifty years

> *The fifty-two-foot Saint Louis Flood Wall*
> *built to handle the 1844 flood*
> *kept water out of downtown*
> *with two feet to spare*

Levees softened
Levees topped
Levees broke

At peak flow the river ran
one million and eighty-thousand
cubic feet per second

After the seven thunders
a voice like a roaring said:

"Go, take the scroll
that is open in the hand
of the angel who is standing
on the sea and on the land"

So I went to the angel and told him
"Give me the little scroll"

"Take it, and eat," the angel said
"It will be bitter to your stomach,
but sweet as honey in your mouth."
I swallowed it and began to speak.

From the plane I see
acres green with corn
hay rolls full of foam
soy swirling and swaying
the tassels poke skyward
from an ancient interior sea

Before the last glacial maximum
when people were thin on the ground

The planet was in drought
and sea levels fell to expose the plains

The great ice sheets
began to melt

We
are the people
who came after
the ice

Can you hear

the American Midwest
inhaling, exhaling?

Do you desire to enter into life
the baptismal question
    to have life in all its abundance?

Earth lodge to sod house to condominium
in less than a hundred years
less than the span
of three generations

    The final poem will be the poem of fact
    in the language of fact
    But it will be the poem of fact
    not realized before[1]

My Gingrich homestead
was one mile east and five miles south
of Riverton, Nebraska

My grandmother
Catherine Helena Gingrich
always remembered and told the story

    Here's where the kitchen was
    Wood stove there

    When wood was too scarce
    we burned cobs and coal

    Smell the dried fruit cookies
    Smell the laundry brought in before rain

---

1. Stevens, Wallace. "Adagia," *Opus Posthumous* (Knopf, 1957)

Her brothers

John Edward Gingrich
Emery Joseph Gingrich
Edward Otto Gingrich
Jeremiah Merle Gingrich

> *The dining room was here,* she said
> *Good place to sit in the winter by the south window*
>
> *Coal-oil stove here*
> *There's where we took Saturday baths*
> *before going to town*
>
> *We moved from the sod house* (where she was born)
> *in aught-seven*
> *or aught-eight*
>
> *The parlor was there*
> *Don't think anyone ever used the front door*
> *One bedroom downstairs*
> *where Grandpa and Grandma slept*

From Listowel, County Kerry
her grandparents, my great-great grandparents

Jeremiah Sullivan
Catherine Mahoney

> *Grandma died in '26*
> *We kids had to empty Grandpa's pot in the morning*
> *Hated that job*
> *The pond's a quarter mile east*
> *Almost hidden by the trees*
> *Dammed it in the '50s*
> *Some government program or federal incentive*

There's natural springs up the draw
No running water in the house
Was cold in the winter
pumping carrying water

No electricity until REA in the '50s
The outhouse was there
Two doors two holes
Cobs and newspaper
Halfway between the house
and the pigs

A second well down there
For the horses
Fruit trees down there too

The blossoms, the tomato jam
We all slept in three bedrooms upstairs
And one bed in the hall

Her sisters
Lucy Anna Gingrich
Mary Velma Gingrich

(O, that legacy of names!)

When sister was in the iron bed
during the storms
she thought she'd be electrocuted
by lightning

Her parents, my great grandparents

Mary Ellen O'Sullivan
Edward Julius Gingrich
(a lock of his mother's hair

braided into his watch fob)

> *Mama and Dad slept in the west room*
> *With the feather tick mattress*

> *It's good the house foundation's still here*
> *On so many of the old places*
> *there's nothing left,* Catherine says

Now I am here
the granddaughter
in Saint Louis
for a baptism

> *regeneration through water in word*

Below me
waters do not part

> *Abrahae filios per mare rubrum ...*
> *You brought the children of Abraham*
> *through the Red Sea on dry ground*
> *from Pharaoh's slavery you liberated them*
> *to prefigure our baptism ...*
> *an indelible mark of freedom*

Six states face down in summer rain
Stubbed silos crest the surface
Farmhouse roofs crown and push for sky

This liquid skin ruptured by satellite dish

Dead steers float by

Tree tops
> *Silver maples*

American elms
Green ash
Black willows
sway and snap

Have they renounced Satan?
a baptismal scrutiny
Have I renounced him?

Three billion cubic meters
of the Mississippi and her mighty sisters
flow into the Gulf of Mexico
forming a silt plume
that covers twenty-seven hundred square miles
cargoes and caravels below

The final poem will be the poem of fact
in the language of fact

Let me give you an inventory of plastic:
bucket barrel boot
Clorox comb Coke bottle
Dupont Dow Dynachem

Do you renounce Satan?
I do renounce him.

And all his works?
I do renounce them.

And all his pomps?
I do renounce them.

seabirds come inland
gulls and terns perch on flotillas of cars

A baptism, yes
but also: spectacle

Fifty dead
Seventeen thousand miles of American farmland
drowned
like a sack of cats

IV. GOLDEN SCARS

Here in Saint Louis
before the Compromise
telegraph wires ran to ground

Out of the east came a prophecy
off *The Jerseyman*'s printing press

> *time (stop)*
> *and distance (stop)*
> *will be annihilated (stop)*
> *The most distant points*
> *of our country (stop)*
> *will be by the telegraph*
> *brought near (full stop)*
> Samuel Morse: *What hath God wrought?*

Here in Saint Louis
the 1880s railroad debate
defined daily work
for the New American

William Ferguson staked his claim
traded land for fame
and a cornered market
on Florissant

Choose two points

One, Sacramento
a western terminus
The Central Pacific
will build west to east

Another Chicago, Omaha, Saint Louis
an eastern terminus

The Union Pacific
will build east to west

Who will ride the Iron Horse
to the finish line?

tallgrass prairie and buffalo
for five thousand years

Pawnee, Ponca, Arapaho
Shawnee, Winnebago, Cheyenne
Kiowa, Comanche, Oceti Sakowan
council fires burning

> General Sherman to President Grant
> *we are not going to let thieving*
> *ragged Indians check and stop*
> *our progress*

Thunderheads get in formation
as far as the eye can see

> *The measure of land*
> *is the measure of our bodies*

Dreamers stare dry-eyed into the sun
reach for the edge of that sword

> *Wakan-Tanka be merciful to me*
> *We want to live!*
> *That is why we are doing this*
> *They say that a herd of buffalo is coming*
> *Now they are here!*
> *The power of the buffalo is coming upon us*
> *Now it is here!*

Transcontinental Big Four
Huntington Stanford Crocker Hopkins
(O, that legacy)

> Charley Crocker also dreams:
> *Mine eye prophetic pierces through the mists*
> *That cloud the future, and I seem to see*
> *A well-devised and executed scheme*
> *Of wholesale robbery within the law*
> *(Made by ourselves)—great, permanent, sublime,*
> *And strong to grapple with the public throat—*
> *Shaking the stuffing from the public purse,*
> *The tears from bankrupt merchants' eyes, the blood*
> *From widows' famished carcasses, the bread*
> *From orphans' mouths!*

In high desert sage
at Promontory Point Utah
in the alkali flats
at Camp Dead Fall

men and metal
    meet
men and metal

Arid as the mind of Carnegie
Divine as a golden spike

> *Lo, soul, seest thou not God's purpose from the first?*
> *The earth to be spann'd, connected by network*
> *The races neighbors to marry and be given in marriage*
> *The oceans to be cross'd the distant brought near*
> *The lands to be welded together*

How did we enter
the American West?

Ex ab ea immunde spiritus
et da locum spiritui sancto

Muleskinner and bullwhacker
'49er and Buffalo gal
all met up at Salt Lake Cutoff

West of Omaha
there were no Sundays

Drive steel
Lay track
Mind the riding boss

Pick-and-shovel coolies
Charley Crocker's pets

Saw ties
Blast rock
Split cottonwood with oak

Central Pacific Railroad
never kept records of
coolie casualties

Track layers
Iron handlers
Hauling crews
Gandy dancers

In camps
Chinese set up joss houses

Buddhist shrines
waited for the summer solstice

> *The way is long*
> *the body overburdened*
> *hungry, he walks home*
> *a thousand li tearing his hair*
> *sobbing before his city walls*
> *the autumn wind*
> *pierces his golden scars*

Up the grade
these *celestial sojourners*
were *bridge monkeys*
mountain tamers

> *Chinese records say in 450 A.D.*
> *five Buddhist beggar priests*
> *traveled the Pacific coast*
> *from British Columbia to Baja*

The most distant points annihilated (stop)
At Cochetopa Pass
At California's Cape Horn

> *Hung suspended in baskets*
> *two thousand feet*
> *above the American River*
> *Chinese drilled and blasted*
> *eight inches of Sierra granite a day*

Red string tied to ti leaves and barley
passed along the line
This is the day of 10,000 heroes

when even shall emperors rest

Never did we enter the West on bended knee
nor set before the mind of God
the labors and occupations of the past

> *Introibemus*
> *ad altare Dei*

Judge us not too harshly
Ute and Paiute
Shoshone and Cheyenne
Galway rail rider
and miner from Yangtze, Guangdong

In Saint Louis
that great gate
was bent like a spoon
by the mind of Eero Saarinen

> *Introibemus*
> *vitae spiritualis*
> *ianua*

A parlor trick to amuse and entertain
the amazing Jefferson
who wished to communicate

with the waters
of the Pacific

V. TALKING WATERS

Confidential: Gentlemen of the Senate
Regarding Exploration of the West 1803

First: Encourage the Indian to abandon hunting
and apply them to the raising of stock
to agriculture and domestic manufacture
and thereby prove to themselves that less land and labor
will maintain them better than in their former mode of living

The extensive forests necessary in the hunting life
will then become useless and they will see advantage
in exchanging them for the means of improving their farms
increasing their domestic comforts

Between dreams
in Saint Louis
I pay out glances
through the gateway arch

see whitecaps
wind whipping water
again and again

In this foreshortened view
I think the Pacific
has come to greet me

Gulls cormorants pelicans
soar and drop
through the gateway's glory hole
calling calling

I smell smoke
salmon on a spit
wrapped in red kelp

Never did we bow beneath her living archways
Never fell contrite before her setting sun

Twenty-eight hundred miles from Saint Louis
Boone's Lick to Fort Kearney
on the California Trail

Two hundred and eighty-eight miles
Saint Louis to Bent's Fort on the Santa Fe Trail

We hammered God's six and one
into a wheel rim
bearing wagons west
iron married with oak

In church
a priest swoops his hands
into the baptismal font
brings up sour water

Three drops from his holy fingertips
gather thunderheads on the child

> *The gift of one's body*
> *the highest form of sacrifice*

No one cries out at this Christ-making
Drums do not pound out ceremony
No low dust huddles around the women's feet

Perhaps
though it is entirely uncertain
I see a ripple of belief
cross the bodies of believers
who brood over this child

Is this the place where crying begins?
Is this the place?

Now sung to and seduced from his brothers
a young cedar is stripped before dawn
by the eldest woman

The sun pole suspended

>   *Cedar tree*
>   *Cedar tree*
>
>   *we have it in the center*
>   *we have it in the center*
>
>   *when we dance*
>   *when we dance*
>
>   *we have it in the center*
>   *we have it in the center*
>
>   *Cedar tree*
>   *Cedar tree*

Bark mutilated, cross-notched
a crotch for eagle
spirit hole for Thunderbird

>   *Lumen Christi*
>   *Deo gratias*

This one is mine, dove descendent
My beloved on whom my favor rests

>   *Guato adaga nyaongum*

Guato adaga nyaongum

I scream because I am a bird
I scream because I am a bird

Talyi imahago
Talyi imahago

The boy will rise up
The boy will rise up

It's Sunday
downtown Saint Louis
riverfront abandoned
bright quiet hot

Flat-eyed buildings stand
shoulder to shoulder
waiting
Streets laid straight by master plainsmen
Ninety degree dry heat on every perfect corner

> *Secondly gentlemen: Multiply trading houses among the Indians*
> *and place within their reach those things*
> *which will contribute more to their domestic comfort*
> *than the possession of extensive but uncultivated wilds*

Let us take field glasses
to field level
prairie grasses
now buried
pushed under
turned and tilled

> *We clear grasses and trees*
> *We plow and carve the land*

Two thousand men and women
scrabbling weeds

Along the low wetlands
along the dyke walls

Only the wind
carries
seed names

Big Bluestem and Indian Grass
Switchgrass and Little Bluestem

In leading the Indian to agriculture
to manufactures and civilization
in bringing together their and our settlements
in preparing them ultimately to participate
in the benefits of our governments
I trust and believe we are acting
for their greatest good

The priest
smudges his thumb in chrism
makes the sign of the cross
on my godson's forehead

In nomine Patris et Filii et Spiritus Sancti

With his thumb the Sun Dancer
makes a stripe in blood
across the forehead and lengthwise
on each side of the buffalo skull

The same sacrificial mark

signs the dancer
to say he is adopted
by buffalo
as *hunka*
relative by ceremony

In spring the vast plains heave and roll
like a green ocean
horse and rider upon them
present a remarkable picture
apparently extending into the air
forty-five to sixty feet high

I reach my hand
down
through cold baptismal waters
pushing
the head of this child
toward his false death

And when the waters recede?
When the rivers
again to themselves
become small?

When dry land is
dry land again?

Then houses will go up again
Farmers will till and plant
Fruit trees will fruit
Earth's breathing room again forgotten

Some of my relations
said Short Bull
have no ears
so I have blown them all away

Beyond chiaroscuro church walls
picture clouds race in a blue white sky
then a horn sounds and blasts:
the next flood stage

VI. THIS SPLENDID CITY

I wasn't a conscript to civilization
I volunteered

This letter is to all who serve on the human front
wearing any mask that will get you home

A word: while we are all dying to get out
someone is dying to get in

Disguised as one of us
this one creeps across enemy lines
borders, militarized zones

slips by
in our momentary infatuation with innocence

An instant later sirens blare
yapping jaws snap shut
in that involuntary reflex
peculiar to Herods Caesars Presidents Kings
called: slaughter

    Lumen Christi
    Deo gratias

The bloodbath
always surprises them

They did nothing more
than indicate
a desired outcome

That is all

Quick or slow

subalterns made it so

Children's heads bashed in by rocks
bashed on rocks by hands

Men with hands
grasp rocks
and bash in small heads

It takes
almost no strength

Casual as a broken bird's egg

Casual as holding down a tiny face
in two inches of water

This is to you
who wake up every morning on the human front
where each one ticks like a clock
waiting to go off
where each one talks like a bomb

This is to you
who wake up in the land
where young ones cut their graceful arms
rake a gilded god-claw on tender flesh

Four men and one woman
fast for forty days

In the end
they sleep only on a bed of sage
take only weak tea

Believe me
I have seen this

When buffalo calls
they enter the sun circle

They thank the sun pole
majestic strong humble

Arbol de vida
entre el corazon del cielo
y corazon de la tierra

You are a way
for our prayers
to travel

With a sharp bone knife
the cacique cuts four slits
small impossibly deep
two on the left breast
two on the right

Then threads a length of wood
or bone
through pectoral skin and muscle

a mother pelican
scores her breast
feeds her young
and all who hunger

The dancers
on long leather thongs
harnessed and hauled
to sun pole's crest

Los Indios de ver el desastre que nos havia venido
y el desastre en que estabamos con tanta desventura
i miseria se sentaron entre nosotros: i con el gran dolor

i lastima que ovieron de vernos en tanta fortuna
començaron todos a llorar recivio tan de verdad
que lexos de alli se podia oíri esto les duró
mas de media hora:
i cierto, ver que estos Hombres
tan fin raçon, i tan crudos
a manera de Brutos
se dolian tanto de nosotros hiço que en mí
i en otros de la compañía cresciese mas la pasión
i la consideracion de nuestra desdicha

And they dance

Blood and water flow

With bowed heads
they run toward the cedar
with all human strength
hurl themselves backward

    And give me the same sentiments
    I ought to have had on Mount Calvary
    had I been an eyewitness of that bloody sacrifice

I hear snapping
as they hang
at apogee at perigee

Their breath bellows out

    Lumen Christi
    Deo gratias

And the people dance
Ecstatic in spirit and truth

This is to you
rag-pickers and bag-jiggers
who bathe in fountains at the feet of generals

And to you
shop clerk at WalMart Kmart Mini-Mart

who does not imagine herself to be a god

And to you
who hoard your IRAs
with a nail thin chance at life

It appears that we

Homo sapiens

have evolved

The waters receded
and out we crawled
taller now by a head

Homo sapien sapien

Two-tongued we talk only to ourselves
in a language no one else speaks

*We dance our clumsy dance
and sing our sorrowful songs*

No we were not conscripts

*I, our Lord being pleased, will take
at the time of our departure*

six natives for your Highnesses
that they may learn to speak

We volunteered to wield sword scythe stock

    to fill our dumb continent with words

for the greatest good
for the greatest number
for the least fortunate

Still
the Tin Man
holds high his award
for good deeds

A ticking clock in the shape of a heart

    I saw no beast of any kind
    except parrots on this island

At least he has something
to keep him up at night

This is for you
nihilist nephilim
riding shotgun on the civilizing project
who wear ghost shirts
on a crowded bus
and smile bright at children near the front
Winchesters Colts Glocks clickers dynamite
strapped to your chest
all tricked out to a laptop
improvised explosive device

    They claimed the shirt Messiah gave

no bullet could go through
But when the soldiers fired at them
They saw this was not true

You who let another pluck out your eyes
so you wouldn't have to see your own soul

> *No end to this marching*
> *forever and ever*

And to you
anawim, ye little ones
refugees from our badly laid foundations of history
our shifting architecture of moral adjustment

> *It's good the foundation is still here.*

I see you in roll-your-own government lines

> *A l'aurore, armés d'une ardente patience,*
> *nous entrerons aux splendides Villes*

I see you with one limb trapped
under the collapsing façade of the Splendid City

> *There is no going past here*
> *without the bite of fire first*

> *Enter it without being deaf*
> *to the singing beyond*

From the plane, I stare down
on raging rivers
trees a car carport livestock

all rip and explode downstream

A brown and white dog runs
along the softening bank

It barks and whines
A blond-headed girl reaches for the leash

She misses
                    and the bank gives way

            Lumen Christi
            Deo gratias

At Saint Louis, the Mississippi
crested forty-nine-point-six feet in August
with a flow rate
fast enough to fill Busch stadium
in sixty-nine seconds

Grafton Illinois flooded 195 days
Clarksville Missouri 187 days
Winfield Missouri 183 days
Hannibal Missouri 174 days
Quincy Illinois 152 days

Water rises rises
takes its thunder home to the sky

Both girl and dog are sucked under, gone

VII. WHERE CRYING BEGINS

I am
the arch
his perfect monument
to westward expansion

The Mississippi will always have its own way
no engineering skill can persuade it to do otherwise
it has always torn down the petty basketwork of engineers
and poured its giant floods withersoever it chose

My inverted catenary curve
like a heavy chain swinging
between posts
annihilating
both time and distance

Introibemus ad altare Dei

I am
Saarinen's Saint Christopher
bending history
from one brown flowing god
to the next

I guess I was four or five, said my grandmother
So it must have been 1901 or aught-two
Or maybe I was older
And it was aught-three or four

I just got up and looked outside
The sun was up

There they were
Silent

Two men on horses
dirty wearing rags
But the horses were pretty
One deep brown with white spots
The other a deeper red
Maroon with white spots
They glistened in the sun

Look at the slide marks of the Prairie Schooners
dragged against canyon walls

Is this the place where crying begins?
Do we have tears for this?

See the mare's carcass in high grass
See the widowmakers

Two women standing, she said
Long dresses like sacks dirty
Two or three children
My age I guess dirty

One horse had a rack
Or a drag attached to it

I wasn't scared
Curious I guess

Dad and Mama were there
They didn't seem scared
Why should I?

They are Pawnees, Dad said
The only ones around here

Dirty Irish, dirty Indian
And still and still

I have seen their bloody sacrifice

> *Mama said they were hungry*
> *She gave them a bag of cornmeal*
> *Bread*
> *And some of whatever we had*
> *It wasn't much*

> *Then they left*
> *Silent as they'd come*
> *Mama just knew what they needed*
> *She always knew*
> *No one ever said a thing*

William Clark supervised
removal of 81,282 Indians
from the eastern United States
to west of the Mississippi

In this clay house
only ceremony can
season us now

VIII. Mono Lake

Far west of the Mississippi
in a rainshadowed Great Basin
on the backside of Yosemite
lays downtown Lee Vining
and the Dodge City motel

Kutzadika'a women bring their skimming baskets
to collect kutsavi from the lake shallows

They move in autumn to the piñon camps
in the hills above the lake

Through the arch
I come face to face
with the eastern foothills
of these high Sierra
their hungry snows
their swirling passes

We held a council and decided to enjoy a week's holiday
on the borders of the curious lake
Mono it is sometimes called and sometimes
the "Dead Sea of California"

Here every sound connects to every other sound
in the manner of silence

The Sierra Nevada
are an earthwave
breaking for millennia
on the sands of the desert basin
with a Washoe zephyr
shaping the leading edge

Mono Lake lies in a lifeless treeless hideous desert
eight thousand feet above the level of the sea
and is guarded by mountains two thousand feet higher

This solemn silent sail-less sea
this lonely tenant of the loneliest spot on earth
is little graced with the picturesque

Glass Mountain's obsidian and mica
shadowed rills of snow melt
sweep into black Glass Creek

      Lee Vining Creek
      Parker Creek
      Walker Creek
      Rush Creek
      Mill Creek

Where freshwater meets lake lye
calcium carbonate tufa towers form stalagmites
a miracle in water and stone

Mono Lake was born
760,000 years ago

Sixty thousand years ago when the glaciers came
the lake was 7,140 feet above sea level

Thirteen thousand years ago the lake was five times larger
and six times deeper than it is now

It is August in Lee Vining
The pines are quiet
There is snow in the lower passes

There are no fish in Mono Lake
no frogs no snakes no polliwogs
nothing in fact that makes life desirable

Only brine shrimp can live in lye

a white feathery sort of worm

a few brine flies and algae live at the crusted edge

And, of course, the birds

Red-throated Loon
Pacific Loon
Common Loon

Pied-billed Grebe
Horned Grebe
Eared Grebe

Western Grebe
Clark's Grebe
American White Pelican
(Ora pro nobis.)

Half a dozen little mountain brooks
flow into Mono Lake
but not a stream of any kind
flows out

What it does with its surplus water
is a dark and bloody mystery

Brown Pelican
Double-crested Cormorant
Pelagic Cormorant

Magnificent Frigatebird
American Bittern
Least Bittern

Great Blue Heron
Snowy Egret
Cattle Egret

Black-crowned Night-Heron
White-tailed Kite
Mississippi Kite
(Ora pro nobis.)

>   *All around its shores stand*
>   *picturesque turret-looking masses*
>   *and clusters of a whitish coarse-grained rock*

>   *If one breaks off fragments of this rock*
>   *he will find perfectly shaped*
>   *and thoroughly petrified*
>   *gulls' eggs deeply imbedded in the mass*

Sharp-shinned Hawk
Merlin
Peregrine Falcon

Sage Grouse
California Quail
Mountain Quail

Black-necked Stilt
Solitary Sandpiper
Wandering Tattler

Jaegers and gulls and terns and murrelets
Nightjars and swifts and hummingbirds

Stellar jays and scrub jays and the common raven
(Ora pro nobis.)

There are two islands
in Mono Lake

>*Nigit the dark spirit*
>*Pahoa the white spirit*

Mono Lake Indians collected brine flies as a delicacy
and traded with the Yosemite for sea shells

When settlers came they rowed to the islands
broke all the birds' eggs
just to be sure what they collected
was fresh

>*All things have their uses*
>*and their part*
>*and proper place*
>*in Nature's economy*

From Mono Lake to Manzanar
Bridgeport to Bishop to Big Pine
Independence to Inyo

Across Tioga Pass
up the Sierran bajada
over fourteen-thousand-foot peaks
one hundred miles to the Pacific

>*Confidential: Gentlemen of the Senate*
>*Regarding Exploration of the West 1803*

>*An intelligent officer*

with ten or twelve chosen men fit for the enterprise
might explore the whole line even to the Western Ocean
in the course of two summers

Their arms and accoutrements—
some instruments of observation
and light and cheap presents for the Indians
would be all the apparatus they could carry
and with an expectation on their return
of a soldier's portion of land
—would constitute the whole expense

The whole expense
Only in a society of money
may one speak this way

IX. SMALL UNINHABITED ISLANDS

The old ones have told us
all roads lead to the sea

The future ones
tell us, *teleos*
the sea does nothing in vain

> *This rock did not come here by itself*
> *This tree does not stand here of itself*

There will come a time when buckeyes ripen
A time cold wind blows

See the double-crested cormorants
swooning under foamheads
Black oystercatchers
American avocets
Sanderlings

See fishing boats beyond the shearwater
trailing Western grebes

There will be a time when grasses green again
when poppies bloom

There will be a seed time
a bulb time
a time when manzanita reddens

In the antechamber of the Western water temple
there are small uninhabited islands
where Indian pounding rocks
serve as brazen lavers
for initiates to the wheel of the Pacific

CONFESSIONS OF A WESTWARD EXPANSIONIST

Lumen Christi
Deo Gratias

See the air patrol acolytes

Pelecanus occidentalis californicus

They fly low across boat-eaters
flat brown gullet-filled raucous

There will be a time
for gathering acorns
wood from the shore
digging soap root

There will be a time
of Miwok Tamal Yahi
(though never again an Ishi time)

> *That's the only time*
> *I remember any of them coming*
> *The wind was blowing*
> *It always did*
> *They were hungry*
> *Mama gave them food*

Ishi: last man
starving and wrapped
in the only gold left in California
her hills and wild grasses

There will be tule fog time
yellow leaf time
a time of endless rain

In Pomo

there is no word
for famine

Who will be your witness then
you architects of expansion
when you are strapped on the ironbound ledge
your back against the sliding weight of North America?

Who will be left to read the little scroll
written on the hand of the angel
who stands on the sea and on the land?

We asked for mercy, O Lord
You gave us knowledge

It is moments before dawn
In the east, fires are burning

The *ikxareyavs* pull shells over themselves
fall into a purple sleep

In the quiet between crashing waves
ka' co and *cuese* gather in the tidepools
for morning prayer

The good kind sane little animals
of the intertidal zone

Black turban snails
Sea cucumbers
Sea squirts
Sea spiders
Sea hares
Sea lettuce
Owl limpets
(Ora pro nobis.)

It is advisable to look from the tidepool
to the stars and then back to the tide pool again

The *pa' hat* sing off shore
a song one hundred years long
heard from Kushiro to Klamath

The world has come
suddenly apart
split in two
the inhabited and the observed

I watch the wildhorse rocks
riding this edge of the world

In the land of the Western Gate
hay una teología de los robles

Whoever would follow in the way
must walk the via roble

El roble sagrado es
el centro del mundo

From Fort Point to Marin headlands
across flat sharkish waters of the Golden Gate
there is only land world and light world
and a world of wind and breath

Writing reduces dynamic sound
to quiescent space

Dawn flows cool over coastal foothills

With my back against the hard uplift
of the Continental shelf, I sit

Sea fig ice plant coyote brush
Poppies iris lupines
Green fescue lit in the sun to red

    Writing separates the word
    from the living present

A gray harbor seal raises her head
gazes toward shore

Maybe she dreams of salmon
farther up the mouth of the Russian River

Spume flashes cold
Swirls into the low places
on a flat slab of sleeper granite

    There comes a time when what we know as life
    meets and enters what we think of as non-life
    barnacle and rock
    rock and earth
    earth and tree
    tree and rain and air

    The units nestle into the whole
    and are inseparable from it

    But the little animals are found to be changed
    no longer set apart and alone

Higher up the outcrop

tucked in the as-yet-untouched night
beneath a California sagebush

three acorns

I can't see them
I know they are there

A tan bark
black cap
maul oak

The most bitter of these
is maul oak

Above, an old goat trail follows
the lip of the sea bluff

Silvered oak and redwood fence posts
section off generations of *Californios* dairy farms
sold now for their luxury views to the few
who can buy the Pacific horizon
California's new gold
her vistas, her amber light

> *When knowledge gives out as a bridge*
> *we must make up for it with love*

And now
and now

> *Emitte lucem tuam*
> *sancta lucem tuam*
> *et veritatum tuam*

We set before

the mind of God all the labors
and occupations of the past

Judge us now:
Ute and Paiute
Pawnee Shoshone Cheyenne
Gate-of-no-return survivor
Galway rail rider
miner from Yangtze

Now is a season for
ceremonies

In the end it is the fact of the arch
not the myth of the arch
that stands

The small uninhabited islands
not their stories
remain

And we
are so much less
than these

In the end there is only
land world and light world
and us—a thin muscular word
stretched between

Nothing but Love in God's Water

for Charles Edward "Ched" Myers

Credo quia absurdum—Tertullian

I. CONTRARY SAINTS

My name in Spanish is free to leave,
prosperous. An Angeleno

who walked north   *ad ventura*
my own *carnales* walking south

in a line of dead *heyoka* who
laugh their heads off

at my birth announcement

On a backward horse they point me east
where I do not want to go

away from my floating world
such contrary saints

Instead I take a tree and break it
Split it into cedar planks

ask the gods for seahorse spirit

and the strength to ride

wear my own face with great abandon
churlish, full of thunder-light

Below I spied the submarine canyons
otter hides and dolphin eyes

Then my *heyoka* sharpened sticks
dipped them in ash, twisted the tips

In India ink they circled the ground, marked
the place where I stepped off

a road not taken
a rotoscope of this way or that

How do I animate this wild falling life?
Those trickster relatives made a sign:

> "Here is where an unborn man
> fucked a tree and swam from land
>
> Here he wrapped in sweet perfume
> a stinking corpse meant for the tomb.
>
> Remember him."

II. BOOK OPEN

abalone shell, cup of salvation
sits on unfinished pine board

white sage tied with purple
yarn, a book open to this:

The beginning of the good news
about Jesus Christ, the Son of God.

III. Society of Money

In those days I had two friends:
a rejected rock, an abandoned river

One blind but strong, the other lost but free.
One taught me to see, the other to be

And, even though my father died,
I was still in love with the chosen way

Even though . . .

And at night I ate pages of an open book
staring up at the sky snake, listening for his voice

*"There are only two societies in the whole
world. One is the society of the people,*

the other is the society of money."
But rock and river disagree.

*One is the society of money, the other
is the society of earth.*

Hard as it is to believe, said rock, I do.
Wherever you go, said river, there I was.

The wind blew. Coyote coughed.
A launch button in the Pacific changed color.

What am I responsible for? I asked my father.

IV. Coals, Manna

I built a fire with mesquite twigs
pine cones and California fescue.

Circled it with river rocks
Tossed in a handful of magic jimson seeds

and over them breathed a thousand prayers
and one more

Pop! Pop! like bullets in an old movie,
those Lords of Distortion, children

sprouted in the coals, manna
the breadfruit in their mouths,

their mouths spouting Tertullian. All this
even though my father died ...

V. 144,000

Oh yes, I still remember the other pretty thieves
four-horsed and spread-eagle

riding thunder and death through my beloved
California, trading in love diseases

like they owned the place.
Raiding the fat of the land and throwing

pestilent acid in the face of the earth. Those giants
burned *wishtoyo*, the rainbow bridge, and corralled

all the colors into *rancherias, surburbias,*
reservas y carceles. I remember the burning,

foil in fire, the snapping of bones, blue moans.
Hot winds sucked the grapes dry, sparrows

like farmworkers took only dust baths, the sacred
lakes coated in floating fish. Creation groaned.

In those days, even the nopales
shriveled and choked on the language

of drought. Children put prickly

poison to their lips for fantasy or fear. Off the I-5
a strong man found a girl, bound her with duct tape

stuffed her in a shed with metal roof, trafficked
her innocence, auctioned her desperation online.

Board men and crowned priests toasted
the strong man: To a job well done.

This is not an age of dark, but of glare, said the poet.
See the shiny demon-signs grin along the highway.

Out toward the islands I look for the lost bridge.
Where is that rainbow now?

Where is the land for the 144,000? Where the river
to wash the robes, where the star-crowns?

Yes, the strong man held me down.
But I remembered my father

and the wandering Aramean.
For a time
I was still.

VI. How to Be a Fool

Then love

that inescapable sneaker wave
that Always Stronger One

turned my head (o love unbound!) and rolled me.

Only then could I see Helen on her far shore,

a bundle of birch twigs for strength in one hand,
a bouquet of chuchupate for healing in the other.

My love and I will invent a country, I said
Coyote laughed. The crows, impatient

with hubris, found another tree.
But it was a blind man who showed me this

A homeless man who took me in
A murdered man who gave me life

A sage plant who taught me how to be a fool
And I pulled a gold coin from a fish's mouth

the only tribute to be paid, I stacked the rest,
a leaning tower of pesos: *Whosoever will, come*

buy wine and milk. Eat that which is good,
and let your soul delight itself in fatness

I pried open church doors so an untamed wolf
and a poor man could lay down together

I went house to house asking if the one
I sought was there

Then at the corner of Santa Ana and Prospect
I saw a condor on a power pole drying its wings

witness here, witness there
witness witness everywhere

I sold what I had and bought the plot.

Now even the Mason jars glisten, fat with fruit

abalone sits with *tonalamatl* in tannic light

I rest my head on an arroyo stone
careful not to disturb its story-roots:

From the rear of an old station wagon
a woman in a Padres shirt pulls out a Tijuana blanket

shakes the sand and dust to the wind
and wraps it around her, a *rebozo*

I glance up and think, an oak tree
read me history on a day very like today.

She parts the roadside scrub
moves like Miriam down the bank, slipping between

willow and mulefat toward an ephemeral
pool in the river bed. Unclips

her hair, kneels.

"Mother, mother, what do you want?"
whisper the stones, quaking with fright.

Curious fingerlings rise to the surface,
the same pouting question on their lips.

She leans her face over the water
cups her hands, taut ripples.

A drink, she says, I want to drink.

VII. AFTER

The ending here is questionable.
Because I'm leaving out the circus,

songs we thought were lost,
homemade tequila,

and everything that came after
the day you were born.

Notes

1. *God builds and unbuilds Worlds*: From *The Sacred Theory of the Earth* by Thomas Burnet, Chapter VII, 1691.

PROPHECIES FROM THE WATERSHED CONFEDERACY

1. *the crown / o'er the earth melted*: From *Antony and Cleopatra* by Shakespeare

2. The stream Kishon . . . that ancient river, Kishon: See Judges 5:21

3. And Hashem kept his word / to the fish: From Rashi's commentary on Judges 5

4. *abandon your house, abandon what you possess, build a boat instead*: Ferry, *Gilgamesh*, "Tablet 11."

5. Maidu warrior-women / died defending the River of Sorrows.' Hayes, *Lower American River*.

6. the Water Walker. See Mark 6:30-52 and Denise Nadeau's foreword to *Watershed Discipleship* on the Water Walker movement led by Anishinaabe Grandmothers. The author joined Ojibway elder, Sharon Day, on the Potomac River Water Nibi Walk in 2016.

7. *Seek life instead of riches*: Ferry, *Gilgamesh*, "Tablet 11."

CONFESSIONS OF A WESTWARD EXPANSIONIST

I. Cahokia

1. Cahokia: Cahokia, the American Indian city on the Mississippi River near present day St. Louis, was the largest urban complex built during the North American Middle Ages. It rivaled Tenochtitlan in Mexico in size and was larger than London or Paris at the time. According to Timothy R. Pauketat and Susan M. Alt (*Medieval Mississippians*), "In the middle of the eleventh century, just as Europe entered its High Middle Ages, North American Indians in the Mississippi River valley began building their first true city, a place now called Cahokia (plate 1). Soon, new capital towns sprang up throughout what is now the U.S. Southeast. Over each place towered from one to as many as two hundred flat-topped pyramids surmounted by large pole-and-thatch temples, residences, and warehouses of community priests and elites. Hereditary rulers or powerful councils led the citizens of individual provinces, who paid tribute and provisions to their leaders. Provinces rose to power or fell from it as their yearly corn crops and their alliances and wars with neighbors either succeeded or failed. Archaeologists once called these people the Mound Builders, but today we know them simply as the Mississippians. In the early 1500s, Spanish explorers met their descendants in the Southeast—people living in towns, each still centered on one or more earthen pyramids topped with wooden temples and elite houses (chapter 12). In fields and farmsteads surrounding the towns, countryside dwellers grew maize (Indian corn), beans, and squash without the aid of draft animals. These people were all children of Cahokia, and the history of their civilization begins along the Mississippi River."

2. Additionally, the Trappists, a Catholic monastic order, had a monastery and school on the Cahokia mounds between 1809-1813. Garraghan, *Illinois Catholic*, 106-136.

3. *She takes cedar incense—cedar mixed with pine sap and sage*: Evelyne Voelker, a Comanche and executive director of the American Indian Center of Mid-America in St. Louis, Mo., performed purification blessings at Cahokia when archaeologists began a dig. Seppa, *Washington Post* (March 12, 1997).

4. hero and hawk: See Townsend, *Hero, Hawk, and Open Hand.*

5. *Earth and myself are of one mind:* "That which I have great affection for, I have no reason or wish to dispose of; if I did, where would I be? The earth and myself are of one mind. The measure of the land and the measure of our bodies are the same. Say to us, if you can say it, that you were sent by the Creative Power to talk to us. Perhaps you think the Creator sent you here to dispose of us as you see fit. If I thought you were sent by the Creator I might be induced to think you had a right to dispose of me. Do not misunderstand me, but understand me fully with reference to my affection for the land. I never said the land was mind to do with as I choose. The one who has the right to dispose of it is the one who has created it. I claim a right to live on my land, and accord you the privilege to live on yours."—Nez Perce leader Hin-mah-too-yah-lat-kekt (Thunder Rolling Down the Mountain, widely known as Chief Joseph, or Joseph the Younger). Humphrey, *The Indian Dispossessed,* 105.

6. *Thou shalt sprinkle me with hyssop:* This psalm is numbered 50 in the Douay Rheims Bible, a translation from the Latin Vulgate first completed for the Roman Catholic Church in 1609. In newer translations, this psalm is numbered 51.

II. FOUR ANGELS

1. Architect Eero Saarinen designed the 630-foot stainless steel arch in St. Louis, Missouri, ("Gateway to the West") as a perfect monument to the spirit of the western pioneers and Thomas Jefferson's vision of westward expansion and manifest destiny. Constructed between 1961-1966, the name of the national park that hosts the arch changed from the Jefferson National Expansion Memorial to the Gateway Arch National Park.

2. a view to space through Thomas Jefferson's panopticon: In 1787, British philosopher and social theorist Jeremy Bentham designed a type of prison in which a single guard could randomly see every prisoner on the principle that if prisoners believed they were constantly watched they would become more compliant. The Panopticon designed by Jeremy Bentham was intended to facilitate the total control and surveillance of prisoners with the least possible input of human energy. Bentham's theories of architecture and social control greatly

influenced Thomas Jefferson. In *The Works of Jeremy Bentham Vol 4*, Bentham described the Panopticon as "a new mode of obtaining power of mind over mind." Jefferson received a copy of Bentham's work in 1792 and experimented with the design in prison architecture as well as Jefferson's influential rotunda motif. Jefferson also explored the panopticon theory in the layout of plantations made profitable by a secured force of enslaved laborers. In *Constructing the Panopticon: Perceptions of Wilderness, Methods of Domination, and the Colonization of Native America*, Jeffrey D. Hendricks writes: "For Jefferson, in terms of his perceptions of wilderness, the central struggle of mankind was to use human power to transform wilderness and recreate the garden of paradise on earth. It is a classic example of belief in the progress narrative, whereby each advancement in civilization brings humanity closer to regaining paradise on earth."

3. *Confidential: Gentlemen of the Senate:* In this secret message of January 18, 1803, President Jefferson asked Congress for $2,500 to explore the West—all the way to the Pacific Ocean. At the time, the territory did not belong to the United States. Congress agreed to fund the expedition that would be led by Meriwether Lewis and William Clark. Jefferson, National Archives, January 18, 1803.

4. *Dred (his name) of color:* Dred Scott marked his name on the court papers with an "X" and his legal representation wrote his name around it. Dred Scott and Harriett Robinson were the central figures when he petitioned the St. Louis Circuit Court for his freedom in April 1846. Although he briefly won freedom on the basis of his former residence in Illinois and Wisconsin territory, appeals to the Missouri Supreme Court by his owner Irene Emerson returned him to slavery in 1852. His advocates refused to accept the decision as final. In 1854, a new freedom suit was filed in the U.S. Circuit Court in St. Louis, but a federal jury upheld the Missouri ruling. Dred Scott appealed that decision to the U.S. Supreme Court. By now the case had moved from being a routine freedom suit to a case of enormous importance because of the national debate over the fate of slavery in the western territories acquired from Mexico. On March 6, 1857, after eleven years of litigation, the Supreme Court, led by Justice Roger B. Taney, denied Dred Scott his freedom, claiming that neither free black nor enslaved persons had rights in the United States and Congress had no right to prevent the spread of slavery. The inflammatory pro-slavery decision nullified the

Missouri Compromise of 1820 (which was legislation that restricted slavery in certain territories) as unconstitutional, and contributed to the sectional strife in the 1850s that led to the Civil War. Scott, *State of Missouri*, Archival Division.

5. *The good rain knows its seasons:* Tu Fu, *Literary Review*, 604.

6. *Dred Scott Born about 1799:* Epitaph on Dred Scott's tombstone. He is buried in Calvary Cemetery in Saint Louis, Missouri.

7. *A slave is not property in the sense:* Canetti, *Crowds and Power*, 383.

8. *Soldier explorer statesman and patriot:* From William Clark's tombstone, Bellefontaine Cemetery, Saint Louis, Missouri.

9. York: A man who was enslaved by William Clark and took part in the Lewis and Clark Corps of Discovery Expedition (1804-1806). See Betts' *In Search of York* and Walker's *Buffalo Dance*.

10. Agaidika Sacajawea: Agaidika, the salmon-eating Shoshone, now known as the Lehmi Shoshone, are the people from whom Sacajawea was stolen in a raid by the Hidatsa when she was 13. She was later enslaved by a French Canadian Catholic fur trader, Toussaint Charbonneau. Charbonneau was hired by Lewis and Clark as an interpreter and took Sacajawea with him. See the work of Rozina George, the great-great-great niece of Sacajawea and cofounder of the Sacajawea Interpretive Center in Salmon, Idaho.

11. *I ate:* William Clark's expedition journals, "Saturday 30th of November 1805."

12. *They should be good servants and intelligent:* The ship's recorder for Christopher Columbus entered in his journal on Thursday, October 11, 1492, the following: "They should be good servants and intelligent, for I observed that they quickly took in what was said to them, and I believe that they would easily be made Christians, as it appeared to me that they had no religion. I, our Lord being pleased, will take hence, at the time of my departure six natives for your Highnesses, that they may learn to speak. I saw no beast of any kind except parrots, on this island." Christopher Columbus, *The New World*, "Landfall," Book 2, Chapter XIV.

13. *The four angels bound:* "Saying to the sixth angel which had the trumpet, Loose the four angels which are bound in the great river

Euphrates. And the four angels were loosed, which were prepared for an hour, and a day, and a month, and a year, for to slay the third part of men."—Revelation 9:14-15

III. Flood Stage

1. *Roll, Jordan, roll:* An African American resistance song meditating on the biblical image of the Jordan River. "Roll, Jordan, roll. Roll, Jordan, roll. I want to go to Heaven when I die to hear old Jordan roll. O brother, you ought to've been there, Yes my Lord, a-sitting up in the Kingdom to hear old Jordan roll. O sister, you ought to've been there, Yes my Lord, a-sitting up in the Kingdom to hear old Jordan roll . O preacher, you ought to've been there, Yes my Lord, a-sitting up in the Kingdom to hear old Jordan roll. O sinner, you ought to've been there, Yes my Lord, a-sitting up in the Kingdom to hear old Jordan roll."

2. *The fifty-two foot Saint Louis Flood Wall:* National Weather Service Forecast Office

3. *Go, take the scroll:* Revelation 10:8-11

4. *Before the last glacial maximum:* Mithen, *After the Ice*, 3-4.

5. *Do you desire to enter into life:* Roman Catholic baptismal rite

6. *The final poem will be the poem of fact:* Stevens, "Adagia."

7. *Catherine Helena Gingrich:* Berger, John H. Unpublished manuscript. "The Gingrich Homestead." The quotes are in the voice of Catherine Helena Gingrich Berger, the author's paternal grandmother.

8. *A regeneration through water in word:* Roman Catholic Catechism II on baptism

9. *Abrahae filios per mare rubrum:* (Latin) From the Roman Missal, Easter Vigil 42 (Blessing of Baptismal Water). "You freed the children of Abraham from the slavery of Pharaoh, bringing them dry-shod through the waters of the Red Sea, to be an image of the people set free in Baptism."

10. *Have they renounced Satan?:* Traditionally, the Roman Catholic baptismal rite begins with the renunciation of Satan. "Do you renounce Satan, father of sin and prince of darkness? And all his works? And all his pomps? And all his empty promises? Do you reject sin, so as to live

in the freedom of God's children? Do you reject the glamour of evil, and refuse to be mastered by sin?" According to the fourth-century bishop Cyril of Jerusalem, the candidate for baptism approaches the baptistery in darkness, turn toward the west where the Prince of Darkness resides, and cry out, "I renounce you, Satan!" before facing east to profess the creed.

11. *Do you renounce Satan?:* ibid.

IV. GOLDEN SCARS

1. *What hath God wrought?:* The Jerseyman newspaper reported that "Time and distance are annihilated, and the most distant points of the country are by its means brought into the nearest neighborhood" by Morse and Vail's 1838 invention of the telegraph. Morse's first telegram said: "What God hath wrought." Barth, *History of Inventing.* The rest of the quote, traditionally used in marriage ceremonies, is "let no man put asunder."

2. *Wakan-Tanka be merciful:* Lawrence, *Society and Animals*, 17-37.

3. *Mine eye prophetic pierces through the mists*: From a political farce written by Ambrose Bierce in 1892. Bierce, *Black Beetles in Amber*, "The Birth of the Rail."

4. *Lo, soul, seest thou not God's purpose from the first?:* Whitman, "Passage to India," 163. In 1869, two events changed global economics. In May the American transcontinental railroad was completed. In November, the Suez Canal opened in Egypt, creating an opening between the Mediterranean Sea and the Red Sea. American poet Walt Whitman explores the catalytic potential when modern science melds with "bibles," "religions," and "temples" of both the East and the West. Whitman's free verse contains the expansive Euro-American vision of expansion and destiny. In "'Strange fascination': Walt Whitman, Imperialism, and the South" (81-95), Wendy Kurant writes, "Whitman was not a stranger to imperialist rhetoric. . . . [David] Simpson notes that transcendental philosophy itself 'makes such [imperialist] gestures both feasible and explicable.' [George] Handley points to Adamic longing expressed through Hegelian dialectic: The figure of Adam appeals to a desire for innocence in approaching and naming

the world so as to ensure a New World originality and authenticity. Such yearning for a complete break from the Old World has paradoxically fostered a Hegelian belief in the inevitable and utterly reliable directive of Western history and a paradoxical lack of interest in social and environmental particulars."

5. *Ex ab ea, immunde spiritus:* (Latin) "Go forth from her, unclean spirit, and give place to the Holy Spirit."

6. *Pick-and-shovel coolies:* Howard, *Great Iron Trail,* 230. "Coolie" was a bureaucratic term for indentured laborers used by the British in colonizing India. The word entered the English language in the 1830s as the indentured labor system gained currency as a replacement for the use of slavery in the British Empire and in the expanding United States. In the mouths of the colonialists, it became a derogatory racial slur against East and South Asians. Companies like the Central Pacific Railroad Company signed laborers to five-year contracts because the Chinese and Irish workers would labor for low wages and live in substandard living conditions. They were targeted by politicians, leaders of organized labor, and Americans who believed the foreign laborers were depressing wages and unfairly taking jobs. In 1858, California passed the first law "to prevent the further immigration of Chinese or Mongolian to this state" (Ninth Session, California Legislature, April 26, 1858).

7. *The way is long:* Lu Lun, "On Meeting a Sick Soldier," *White Pony,* 231. While Robert Payne worked with Chinese scholars for translation to English in *White Pony,* he is considered a "sinicized Westerner" whose aim was to introduce Chinese poetry to the West and reflect Western sensibilities. For translations of Chinese poetry in English by Chinese scholars and translators, see *Sunflower Splendor: Three Thousand Years of Chinese Poetry,* edited by Wu-chi Liu nd Irving Yucheng Lo.

8. *Chinese records say in 450 A.D.:* "The Chinese, or Celestials (from the Celestial Empire), as they were often called in the 1800s, have a long history in Western America. Chinese records indicate that Buddhist priests traveled down the west coast from present day British Columbia to Baja California in 450 A.D. Spanish records show that there were Chinese ship builders in lower California between 1541 and 1746. When the first Anglo-Americans arrived in Los Angeles, they found Chinese shopkeepers." Chugg, *Brown Quarterly 1.*

9. *celestial sojourners:* A phrase used by Paul G. Chase and William S. Evans Jr. in their 1969 paper "Celestial Sojourners in the High Sierras: The Ethno-Archaeology of Chinese Railroad Workers (1865–1868) to describe Chinese immigrants. "Celestial" refers to citizens of the "celestial empire" of China, an empire ruled by the dictates of heaven. But "celestial" became a pejorative description when used by the Americans.

10. *Hung suspended in baskets:* "At Cape Horn in the Sierras, they hung suspended in baskets 2,000 ft. above the American River below them and drilled and blasted a road bed for the railroad without losing a single life (lots of fingers and hands though). After hitting the Nevada desert they averaged more than a mile a day. But working in 120 heat and breathing alkali dust took its toll. Most were bleeding constantly from the lung." Chugg.

11. *Red string tied to ti leaves and barley:* Just after the summer solstice in 1867, Chinese railroad workers went on strike against the unjust labor practices of the Central Pacific Railroad. They sent messages to each other using a special knot for tying tea leaves together. It was the largest labor action in the country at that time. After nine days, the strike ended when Central Pacific director Charles Croker cut off all food, supplies, and transportation to the Chinese work camps. See *China Men* by Maxine Hong Kingston and The Chinese Railroad Workers in North America Project at Stanford University.

12. *Introibemus vitae spiritualis ianua:* (Latin) "We will go to the archway of life in the Spirit." Roman Catholic Catechism II on baptism.

V. TALKING WATERS

1. *Confidential: Gentlemen of the Senate:* Jefferson, National Archives, January 18, 1803.

2. *Boone's Lick to Ft. Kearney:* Stops along the Sacramento and Santa Fe trails of European immigrant westward migration in the mid-1800s.

3. *Bent's Fort to Santa Fe:* ibid.

4. *Lumen Christi:* (Latin) "The Light of Christ." Roman Missal, Easter Vigil 42.

5. *Is this the place where crying begins:* "A-nea thibiwa hana, A-nea thibiwa hana,—Thi aya ne, Thi aya ne" is a Sioux song sung in the sweat lodge. "The place where crying begins, the place where crying begins—the death mound, the death mound." The sweat lodge is a place associated with tears. Mooney, *Ghost Dance*, 231.

6. *Cedar tree:* Similar to the Ghost Dance, the Sun Dance is celebrated around a tree set up in in the center of a circle. The cedar tree is sacred in many Native traditions. Mooney, 228.

7. *Guato adaga nyaongum:* "This song was composed by Pa-guadal, 'Red Buffalo,' at a Ghost dance held on Walnut creek in the summer of 1893, under the direction of the prophet Pa-ingya, for the purpose of resurrecting Red Buffalo's son, who had recently died." Mooney, 314-15.

8. *Secondly: to multiply trading houses among the Indians:* Jefferson, National Archives, January, 18, 1803.

9. *We clear grasses and trees:* "Clearing the Fields" from The Book of Songs. *White Pony*, 39.

10. *In leading the Indian to agriculture, to manufactures, and civilization:* Jefferson, National Archives, January, 18, 1803.

11. *In nomine Patris, et Filii, et Spiritus Sancti:* (Latin) "In the name of the Father, and the Son, and the Holy Spirit." Roman Catholic Missal.

12. *In spring, the vast plain heaves and rolls:* "The Great Prairie Highway." National Park Service Santa Fe National Historic Trail brochure.

13. *Some of my relations:* From a sermon delivered by Short Bull, a Sioux resistance leader, at Red Leaf camp on Pine Ridge Reservation, October 31, 1890, after he visited Wovoka, the messiah who brought the Ghost Dance. Short Bull's sermon was moving closer the time table when God would bring the next world (one without whites) into existence. "My friends and relations: I will soon start this thing in running order. I have told you that this would come to pass in two seasons, but since the whites are interfering so much, I will advance the time from what my father above told me to do, so the time will be shorter. Therefore you must not be afraid of anything. Some of my relations have no ears, so I will have them blown away." Mooney, Ghost Dance, 30-1. The final phrase is reminiscent of the biblical phrase, "Those who have ears, let them hear" (Matthew 13:9, Revelation 2:17, 3:13).

VI. THE SPLENDID CITY

1. *Arbol de vida:* (Spanish) "Tree of life between the heart of the sky and the heart of the land . . . you are a way for our prayers to travel on." I heard this prayer from Esteban Pop, a Guatemalan Maya-Quiche elder, honoring the sun pole on Tayac Piscataway land near Port Tobacco, Maryland, in September 2004. The elders were visiting for the opening of the Smithsonian's National Museum of the American Indian in Washington, D.C.

2. *Los Indios de vèr el desastre que nos havia venido:* "Upon seeing the disaster we had suffered, our misery and distress, the Indians sat down with us and all began to weep out of compassion for our misfortune, and for more than half an hour they wept so loud and so sincerely that it could be heard far away. Verily, to see beings so devoid of reason, untutored, so like unto brutes, yet so deeply moved by pity for us, it increased my feelings and those of others in my company for our own misfortune."—Cabeza De Vaca, Chapter XII.

3. *who does not imagine herself to be a god:* Neruda, "Towards the Splendid City," December 13, 1971. Permission from (c) The Nobel Foundation.

4. *We dance our clumsy dance:* ibid.

5. *I, our Lord being pleased, will take:* The ship's recorder for Christopher Columbus entered in his journal on Thursday, October 11, 1492, the following: "They should be good servants and intelligent, for I observed that they quickly took in what was said to them, and I believe that they would easily be made Christians, as it appeared to me that they had no religion. I, our Lord being pleased, will take hence, at the time of my departure six natives for your Highnesses, that they may learn to speak. I saw no beast of any kind except parrots, on this island." Christopher Columbus, *New World*, "Landfall," Book 2, Chapter XIV.

6. *fill our dumb continent with words:* Neruda, "Towards the Splendid City."

7. *I saw no beast of any kind:* The ship's recorder for Christopher Columbus entered in his journal on Thursday, October 11, 1492, the following: "They should be good servants and intelligent, for I observed that they quickly took in what was said to them, and I believe that

they would easily be made Christians, as it appeared to me that they had no religion. I, our Lord being pleased, will take hence, at the time of my departure six natives for your Highnesses, that they may learn to speak. I saw no beast of any kind except parrots, on this island." Christopher Columbus, *New World*, "Landfall," Book 2, Chapter XIV.

8. *They claimed the shirt Messiah gave*: A chorus from "The Indian Ghost Dance and War" song written by "colored private troop" W. H. Prather, Troop I, 9th Cavalry. It became a classic of the barracks and was used to pump up the soldiers before the massacre of the Sioux at Wounded Knee and in putting down Indian rebellions in Nebraska. Mooney, Ghost Dance, 136-37.

9. *No end to this marching*: Nineteen Han poems. *White Pony*, 107.

10. *A l'aurore, armes d'une ardente patience*: (French) "In the dawn, armed with a burning patience, we shall enter the splendid Cities." A quote from Rimbaud. Neruda, "Towards the Splendid City."

11. *There is no going past here*: Dante, *Purgatorio*, trans. W.S. Merwin, 27.10-12.

VII. WHERE CRYING BEGINS

1. *The Mississippi River will always have its own way*: "The Mississippi will always have its own way; no engineering skill can persuade it to do otherwise; it has always torn down the petty basketwork of the engineers and poured its giant floods whithersoever it chose, and will continue to do this." Twain, *Eruption*.

2. *Introibemus ad altare Dei*: (Latin) "We will go unto the altar of the Lord."

3. *Saarinen's Saint Christopher*: St. Christopher is the "Christ-bearer" pictured carrying the Child Christ over a mighty river.

4. *I guess I was four or five*: Berger, John H. Unpublished manuscript. "On Visiting the Pawnee Indian Museum in Northern Kansas: Catherine Helena Gingrich Berger Remembers."

5. *Is this the place where crying begins*: "A-nea thibiwa hana, A-nea thibiwa hana—Thi aya ne, Thi aya ne" is a Sioux song sung in the sweat lodge. "The place where crying begins, The place where crying begins—the

death mound, the death mound." The sweat lodge is a place associated with tears, solidarity, cleansing, healing. Mooney, *Ghost Dance*, 231.

6. *Do we have tears for this?*: "He halted. As he wept, he cried: 'Achates, where on this earth is there a land, a place that does not know our sorrows? Look! There is Priam! Here, too, the honorable find its due and there are tears for passing things; here, too, things mortal touch the mind. Forget your fears; this fame will bring you some deliverance.' He speaks. With many tears and sighs he feeds his soul on what is nothing but a picture." *The Aeneid of Virgil*, translated by Allen Mandelbaum, 17.

7. *Two women standing*: Berger, John H. Unpublished manuscript. "On the Pawnee Indian Museum in Northern Kansas: Catherine Helena Gingrich Berger Remembers."

8. *Mama said they were hungry*: ibid.

VIII. MONO LAKE

1. *Kutzadika'a women*: Mono Lake Committee, "Kutzadika'a People."

2. *We held a council*: "We held a council and decided to make the best of our misfortune and enjoy a week's holiday on the borders of the curious Lake. Mono, it is sometimes called, and sometimes the 'Dead Sea of California.'" Twain, *Roughing It*, Chapter 37.

3. *Mono Lake lies in a lifeless treeless hideous desert*: "Mono Lake lies in a lifeless, treeless, hideous desert, eight thousand feet above the level of the sea, and is guarded by mountains two thousand feet higher, whose summits are always clothed in clouds. This solemn, silent, sail-less sea—this lonely tenant of the loneliest spot on earth—is little graced with the picturesque." ibid, Chapter 38.

4. *Mono Lake formed*: Mono Lake Committee, "The Natural History."

5. *There are no fish in Mono Lake*: "There are no fish in Mono Lake—no frogs, no snakes, no polliwigs—nothing, in fact, that goes to make life desirable." Twain, *Roughing It*, Chapter 38.

6. *a white feathery sort of worm*: "Millions of wild ducks and sea-gulls swim about the surface, but no living thing exists under the surface,

except a white feathery sort of worm, one half an inch long, which looks like a bit of white thread frayed out at the sides." ibid.

7. *Half a dozen little mountain brooks:* "Half a dozen little mountain brooks flow into Mono Lake, but not a stream of any kind flows out of it. It neither rises nor falls, apparently, and what it does with its surplus water is a dark and bloody mystery." ibid.

8. *All around its shores stand:* "In speaking of the peculiarities of Mono Lake, I ought to have mentioned that at intervals all around its shores stand picturesque turret-looking masses and clusters of a whitish, coarse-grained rock that resembles inferior mortar dried hard; and if one breaks off fragments of this rock he will find perfectly shaped and thoroughly petrified gulls' eggs deeply imbedded in the mass." ibid, Chapter 39.

9. *Nigit the dark spirit:* From author's personal notes after spending a few weeks assisting in brine shrimp research in Mono Lake during the summer of 1984.

10. *All things have their uses:* Twain, *Roughing It*, Chapter 38.

11. *Confidential: Gentlemen of the Senate:* Jefferson, National Archives, January 18, 1803.

IX. Small Uninhabited Islands

1. *This rock did not come here by itself:* "This rock did not come here by itself. This tree does not stand here of itself. There is one who made all this, Who shows us everything." Yuki initiation song. *Literature of California*, 37.

2. *The brazen laver:* A symbol from ancient baptism rituals that, after bringing one's sacrifice to the altar, a candidate would wash in the brazen laver, typically filled with seawater, in order to be cleansed and to prepare one for entry into the Temple or sacred grove.

3. *Miwok Tamal Yahi:* Traditional peoples of California.

4. *Ishi:* On August 28, 1911, the last "wild Indian" in the United States, a Yahi man, came out of the California hills. He was starving. He called himself "Ishi" for "last man." See Kroeber, *Ishi in Two Worlds*. For a

Catholic theological perspective on these events and other essays on Native Americans, see Merton, *Ishi Means Man*.

5. *That's the only time I remember any coming*: Berger, John H. Unpublished manuscript. "On Visiting the Pawnee Indian Museum in Northern Kansas: Catherine Helena Gingrich Berger Remembers."

6. *In Pomo*: "Sonoma County's resources were plentiful enough that the Pomo language had no word for famine—in fact, the only plant they ever felt it necessary to cultivate was the tobacco they used in spiritual ceremonies." Winegarner, *Sacred Sonoma*, Chapter 2.

7. *ikxareyavs*: (Pomo) "spirit people." Harrington, *Bureau of American Ethnography*, No.7. Also includes information on the Pomo culture of acorns.

8. *ka' co*: (Chumash) "abalone people." Used with permission from Monique Sonoquie, founder of the Indigenous Youth Foundation, drawn from *The Beginning of the Chumash*, retold by Monique Sonoquie. Sonoquie used *Chumashan and Costanoan Vocabularies* by H.W. Henshaw (1884-1888) and California Indian Linguistic Record, *The Mission Indian Vocabularies of Alphonse Pinart* (Chumash section), edited by R.F. Heifer, Anthropological Records, Volume 15, No. 2, University of California Press, 1955. 85-202.

9. *cuese*: (Chumash) "starfish people." ibid.

10. *the good, kind, sane little animals*: Ricketts, *Between Pacific Tides*.

11. *It is advisable to look from the tidepool*: Steinbeck, *Log from the Sea of Cortez*,178.

12. *pa' hat*: (Chumash) "whale people." With gratitude to Monique Sonoquie who sent photos of a magnificent whale in the Klamath River that Monique took "several years ago when she came up about a mile into the river. She was right under the bridge and we would stop and sing to her. She would roll on her side as in these photos and look at us while we were singing to her."

13. *The world has come suddenly apart*: "The world has come suddenly apart, split in two, into the inhabited and the observed." Evans, "Graham Greene," *Prospect*.

14. *In the land of the Western Gate*: "In this land of the Western Gate, therefore, 'whoever would follow Jesus must take up' the tree of life

as well, the *via roble*. For the Great Economy is like an acorn which, though small, when pressed into the earth grows up and puts forth large branches. *El roble sagrado al centro del mundo*. By it we can practice *mesticismo*, and in its great canopy 'all the birds of the air can find a nest.'" Myers, *Roll Away the Stone*, Chapter 11.

15. *Writing reduces dynamic sound*: "[Writing] initiated what print and computers only continue, the reduction of dynamic sound to quiescent space, the separation of the word from the living present, where alone spoken words can exist." Ong, *Orality and Literacy*.

16. *Writing separates the word*: "[Writing] initiated what print and computers only continue, the reduction of dynamic sound to quiescent space, the separation of the word from the living present, where alone spoken words can exist." ibid.

17. *There comes a time when what we know as life*: Steinbeck, *Log from the Sea of Cortez*, 178.

18. *When knowledge gives out as a bridge*: "When knowledge gives out as a bridge, we make up for it with love. That is what you have to call it—love." Altree, *Why Talk?*, 35.

19. *Emitte lucem tuam*: (Latin) "Send forth your light, your holy light, and your truth."

NOTHING BUT LOVE IN GOD'S WATER

1. This poem was written to honor Charles Edward "Ched" Myers—biblical scholar, theological animator, and watershed defender—for his 60th birthday. The title of this poem is taken from a version of the Black spiritual "Old Ship of Zion," recorded by The Mighty Wonders of Aquasco, Maryland, in 1971. It's the only known version of the song that uses the line "nothing but love in God's water." The lyrics include: "'Tis the old ship of Zion . . . Step on board if you want to see Jesus . . . Just step on board and follow me . . . There's nothing but love in God's water . . . Just step on board and follow me." Darden, *Nothing But Love*, 124.

I. CONTRARY SAINTS

1. The name Charles comes from the German *karlaz* meaning "free man." The meaning carries over into English in the word *churl*, a husbandman, a layman, a freeman of the lowest class. Edward means guardian of prosperity. And the name Myers came to denote a tenant farmer or, in the Jewish lineages, *meir*, one who enlightens.

2. *carnales*: A Spanish slang word for those you are closest to, your "blood."

3. *heyoka*: Among the Lakota, they are the contrarians, jesters, fools, or sacred clowns. In Christian tradition, in Paul's first letter to the Corinthians (4:10) Paul identifies himself as a "fool for Christ."

4. rotoscoping: An animation technique in which animators trace over footage, frame by frame, for use in live-action and animated films. See Ched Myers' affinity for cartoonist Max Fleischer and Koko the clown, which leads Myers to use the language of "theological animation" and "animating" a social movement.

5. "Remember him." See Mark 14:8-9 on the one who anointed Jesus' body.

II. BOOK OPEN

1. The beginning of the good news about Jesus Christ, the Son of God. Mark 1:1

III. SOCIETY OF MONEY

1. Even though my father died: Edward Allan Myers Jr. died on Feb. 17, 1991. He was a fifth-generation native Californian and a member of the historical association E Clampus Vitus. He was survived by his wife of 46 years, Charlotte Myers of Laguna Niguel, and five children, including Ched, and five grandchildren. Myers dedicated *Who Will Roll Away the Stone?* to his father.

2. sky snake: The Chumash believe that Sky Snake is the Milky Way and gave the people the gift of fire, according to Chumash elder Julie

Tumamait-Stenslie, tribal leader of the Barbareño/Ventureño band of Mission Indians (BVBMI) in Ojai, California.

3. A launch button in the Pacific changed color: Myers worked for many years with the people of the Pacific Rim and south Pacific defending their homelands against colonial invasion from the nuclear nations.

4. "There are only two societies in the whole world. One is the society of the people, the other is the society of money."—Chief Lawrence Ngirturong (Ngaremlengui, Palau). Myers, Aldridge, *Resisting the Serpent*.

IV. Coals, Manna

1. magic jimson seeds: Chumash elders teach that to create the Chumash people, Earth Mother *Hutash* buried the seeds of a magical plant on Santa Cruz Island in the Santa Barbara Channel, off the coast of Southern California. The people sprung full grown from the plant, both men and women, to inhabit the island. The seeds are traditionally associated with jimson weed, *Datura*, of which there is a special religious devotion among the Chumash, according to tribal leader Julie Tumamait-Stenslie.

2. Tertullian: An early Christian writer (155-240 CE) from the region of Tunisia who rejected rationalism and accepted a Gospel that addressed itself to the "non-rational levels of perception." In *De Carne Christi* (V, 4) he writes: "The Son of God was crucified: there is no shame, because it is shameful. And the Son of God died: it is by all means to be believed, because it is absurd. And, buried, He rose again: it is certain, because impossible." The epigraph for this poem—*Credo quia absurdum*—means "I believe because it is absurd," a paraphrase from Tertullian's work. It was also the motto of the historical association E Clampus Vitus to which Myers' father belonged.

V. 144,000

1. four-horsed and spread-eagle: Chumash rock paintings show four mounted horsemen (almost certainly Spanish) from the time of the Conquest. In Christian tradition this echoes eerily the "four horsemen of the apocalypse" identified in Revelation 6:1-8. In Christian

mythology the horsemen represent: Conquest, War, Famine, and Death.

2. trading in love diseases: "The love of possession is a disease with them," said Tatonka Yatonka. Myers, Aldridge, *Resisting the Serpent.*

3. *wishtoyo:* The rainbow bridge. Chumash elders teach that the first name of the Chumash people was *Michumash* (the island people) because the first people lived on the Channel Islands off the coast of California Sur. When the islands became too crowded *Hutash* (Mother Earth) created a bridge from a *wishtoyo*, a rainbow, for the people to walk across to the mainland, according to Chumash tribal leader Julie Tumamait-Stenslie.

4. *rancherias:* Between 1851 and 1852, 18 treaties were negotiated between the U.S. federal government and more than 100 California Indian Tribes and Bands. The Indians ceded their rights to the land and the government promised to pay for the land and secure more than 8 million acres for the native tribes. The U.S. Senate secretly rejected the treaties and the California Indians lost all claims to their land. In the early 1900s, the Northern California Indian Association was formed and eventually petitioned Congress to provide money and lands to Native Americans in California. Congress appropriated money to purchase 9,000 acres of land that became 50 separate *rancherias,* disconnected postage-stamp land parcels to which Indian families were given rights. Miller, "The Secret Treaties with California Indians," *Prologue.*

5. *surburbias:* A district where people live on the outskirts of an urban core, occupied primarily by private residences. Lewis Mumford described American suburban life as "an asylum for the preservation of illusion."

6. *reservas:* A Spanish word for land allotments owned by a federal government in trust for indigenous peoples. In the U.S. these are called "reservations." In Canada, they are called First Nation reserves. In British-ruled Ireland, the Cromwellians proclaimed "To Hell or to Connacht" for native Irish, forcibly removing thousands of Irish to Connacht to keep them penned between the sea and the river Shannon. Cunningham, *Conquest and Land.*

7. *carceles:* A Spanish word for jail or prison.

8. a strong man: See Mark 3:27.

9. found a girl: Bidart, "Herbert White," *In the Western Night.*

10. *This is not an age of dark, but of glare:* Jellema, "A Word in the Glare," *A Slender Grace.*

11. and the wandering Aramean: See Deuteronomy 25:6. See also Corbett, *Sanctuary of All Life* and *Goatwalking.*

VI. How To Be a Fool

1. Always Stronger One: See Luke 11:22.

2. Helen on her far shore: In 1999 Ched Myers married with Elaine Louise Enns, a Canadian Mennonite from Saskatoon, Saskatchewan, with a heritage from the mass migration of Mennonites during the Russian revolution from the region of the Ukraine. (For more, read "Pilgrimage to the Ukraine: Revisioning History through Restorative Justice" by Elaine Enns.) The name Elaine comes from the Greek for Helene meaning "torch" or moon or the unexpected presence of fire (as in St. Elmo's fire). In Greek mythology Helen was the daughter of Zeus and is best known through Homer's *Odyssey* as Helen of Troy.

3. chuchupate: *Lomatium califomicum,* a plant native plant to the West and Southwest, is considered a "virtuous herb" for healing in Chumash tradition. A Chumash quote is "We are constantly walking on herbs, the virtues of which no one knows." Timbrook, "Virtuous Herbs, *Ethnobiology.*

4. *My love and I will invent a country:* A paraphrase. Levis, "In a Country," *The Afterlife,* 30.

5. pulled a gold coin from a fish's mouth: See Matthew 17:27

6. *Whosoever will, come / buy wine and milk:* Isaiah 55:2

7. condor: The California condor (*Gymnogyps californianus*) is the largest bird in North America. Many California Indian traditions, including Chumash, honor the condor through ceremony or, as it is still known in southern California, the Panes festival of the Luiseño.

8. *tonalamatl:* A Nahuatl word for sacred book or literally the "page of days." It refers to an almanac used in Central Mexico prior to the Spanish conquest.

9. *rebozo:* A Spanish word from the verb "to cover or envelop oneself," the *rebozo* is a hand-woven cloth used by Indigenous women in Mexico as a wrap, sling, and cover. In Nahuatl it is called *ciua nequealtla-pacholoni* ("that which touches the woman") or a *cenzotl,* "cloth of a thousand colors."

10. an oak tree / read me history on a day very like today: See *teología de los robles.* Myers, *Roll Away the Stone,* 378-79.

11. Miriam: "Miriam the prophetess" is named in the Talmud as one of seven major female prophets of Israel. See Exodus 2:1-10.

12. A drink, she says, I want a drink.: "And the spirit and the bride say: Come. And he that heareth, let him say: Come. And he that thirsteth, let him come. And he that will, let him take the water of life, freely." Revelation 22:17 (Douay-Rheims Bible)

VII. AFTER

1. The ending here is questionable: Mark 16, between verses 8 and 9. Most scholars say that Mark's gospel ended at 16:8 and that the remaining verses are "questionable." This begs the question: Does Mark's gospel end with the lines "for they were afraid" (verse 8) or with the disciples "confirming the word with signs" (verse 20)? The answer is our existential work. The final section, to complete the sacred number, has not yet been lived.

Bibliography

Altree, Wayne. *Why Talk? A Conversation About Language with Walter Ong.* Novato, CA: Chandler & Sharp, 1973.

The Aeneid of Virgil. Translated by Allen Mandelbaum. Oakland, CA: University of California Press, 1982.

Barth, Linda J. *A History of Inventing in New Jersey: From Thomas Edison to the Ice Cream Cone.* New Jersey: The History Press, 2013.

Berger, John H. Unpublished collection of poems about Catherine Helena Gingrich Berger.

Betts, Robert B. *In Search of York: The Slave Who Went to the Pacific with Lewis and Clark.* University Press of Colorado, 2002.

Bidart, Frank. "Herbert White." In *In the Western Night: Collected Poems:1965-1990.* New York: Farrar, Straus and Giroux, 1991.

Bierce, Ambrose. "The Birth of the Rail." In *Black Beetles in Amber.* San Francisco: Western Author's Publishing, 1892. Project Gutenberg. http://www.gutenberg.org/files/12977/12977.txt

Cabeza de Vaca, Alvar Núñez. From *The Journey of Alvar Nuñez Cabeza De Vaca, 1542.* "CAP. XII. Como los Indios nos truxeron de comer." Project Gutenberg. http://www.gutenberg.net/catalog/world/readfile?fk_files=47812&offset=61347

Canetti, Elias. "Slavery." In *Crowds and Power.* Translated by Carol Stewart. New York: Farrar, Straus and Giroux, 1984.

Charleston, Steven. *The Four Vision Quests of Jesus.* New York: Morehouse Publishing, 2015.

Christopher Columbus and the New World of His Discovery. Translated by Filson Young. Book-2, Chapter XIV, "Landfall." 1906. Project Gutenberg. http://www.nalanda.nitc.ac.in/resources/english/etext-project/travel/colombus/book-2chapter6.html

Chugg, Robert. "The Chinese and the Transcontinental Railroad." *Brown Quarterly 1,* (No. 3, Spring 1997).

Clark, William. "Saturday 30th of November 1805." Journals of the Lewis and Clark Expedition, digital edition. Lincoln, NE: University of Nebraska Press. https://lewisandclarkjournals.unl.edu/item/lc.jrn.1805-11-30

Corbett, Jim. *Sanctuary of All Life: The Cowbalah of Jim Corbett.* Englewood, CO: Howling Dog Press, 2005.

———. *Goatwalking: A Guide to Wildland Living, A Quest for the Peaceable Kingdom.* New York: Viking, 1991.

Cunningham, John. *Conquest and Land in Ireland: The Transplantation to Connacht, 1649-1680.* UK: Royal Historical Society, 2011.

Dante Alighieri. *Purgatorio: A New Verse Translation.* Translated by W.S. Merwin. Port Townsend, WA: Copper Canyon, 2018.

Darden, Robert. *Nothing but Love in God's Water: Volume 1: Black Sacred Music from the Civil War to the Civil Rights Movement.* University Park, PA: Penn State University Press, 2014.

Dred Scott signature on original. Case documents, 1846. Accessed at State of Missouri, Archival Division, Conservation of the Dred Scott Papers. https://www.sos.mo.gov/archives/localrecs/conservation/dredscott/treatment

See State Archives Local Records "Conservation of the Dred Scott Papers" State Capitol, Room 208 and State Information Center, 600 W. Main St. Jefferson City, MO 65101. http://www.sos.mo.gov/archives/localrecs/conservation/dredscott/intro.asp

Dubagio, Sharon. *South America, Mi Hija.* Pittsburgh: University of Pittsburgh Press, 1992.

Enns, Elaine. 2011. "Pilgrimage to the Ukraine: Revisioning History through Restorative Justice." Bartimaeus Cooperative Ministries, Oak View, California. http://www.bcm-net.org/pilgrimage-to-the-ukraine-revisioning-history-through-restorative-justice-elaine-enns

Evans, Julian. "Graham Greene." *Prospect* magazine (Vol. 102. UK, 2004).

Ferry, David. "Tablet 11." *Gilgamesh: A New Rendering in English Verse.* New York: Farrar, Strauss, and Giroux, 1993.

Garraghan, S. J., G. J. "The Trappists of Monk's Mound." *Illinois Catholic Historical Review* (Vol.8, No. 2, 1925). http://penelope.uchicago.edu/Thayer/E/Gazetteer/Places/America/United_States/Illinois/_Texts/journals/IllCHR/8/2/The_Trappists_of_Monks_Mound*.html.

Ghosh, Amitav. *The Great Derangement Climate Change and the Unthinkable.* Chicago: University of Chicago Press, 2016.

"The Great Prairie Highway." National Park Service Santa Fe National Historic Trail brochure. https://www.nps.gov/safe/planyourvisit/brochure_text.htm

Harrington, John P. *Karuk Indian Myths.* Washington, D.C.: Smithsonian Institution Bureau of American Ethnography Bulletin (No. 107, 1932). https://repository.si.edu/bitstream/handle/10088/34579/bae_bulletin_107_Karuk_1932.pdf. "Acorn Maidens"

Hayes, Peter J, ed. *The Lower American River: Prehistory to Parkway.* Sacramento, CA: American River Natural History, 2005.

Heaney, Seamus. *Station Island.* New York: Farrar, Straus and Giroux, 1986.

Hendricks, Jeffrey D. "Constructing the Panopticon: Perceptions of Wilderness, Methods of Domination, and the Colonization of Native America." MA thesis, California State University, Long Beach, 2006.

Hicks, Jack, et al. *The Literature of California: Writings from the Golden State.* Oakland, CA: University of California Press, 2000.

Hong Kingston, Maxine. *China Men.* New York: Alfred A. Knopf, 1980.

Howard, Robert West. *The Great Iron Trail—The Story of the First Transcontinental Railroad.* New York: Bonanza Books, 1962.

Humphrey, Seth King. *The Indian Dispossessed.* Boston: Little, Brown, and Company, 1905.

Jefferson, Thomas. President Thomas Jefferson's confidential message to Congress concerning relations with the Indians, January, 18, 1803; Record Group 233, Records of the United States House of Representatives, HR 7A-D1; National Archives.

Kroeber, Theodora. *Ishi in Two Worlds: A Biography of the Last Wild Indian in North America.* Berkeley: University California Press, 1963.

Kurant, Wendy. "'Strange fascination': Walt Whitman, Imperialism, and the South." *Walt Whitman Quarterly Review 29* (2012). https://doi.org/10.13008/2153-3695.2012

Lawrence, Elizabeth Atwood. "The Symbolic Role of Animals in the Plains Indian Sun Dance." *Society and Animals: Journal of Human-Animal Studies* (Vol. 1, No. 1, 1993).

Levis, Larry. "In a Country." In *The Afterlife.* Pittsburgh: Carnegie Mellon University Press, 1998.

Liu, Wuji and Irving Yucheng Lo, eds. *Sunflower Splendor: Three Thousand Years of Chinese Poetry.* Bloomington, IN: Indiana University Press, 1990.

Lu Lun. "On Meeting a Sick Soldier." In *The White Pony: An Anthology of Chinese Poetry from the Earliest Times to the Present Day, Newly Translated,* edited by Robert Payne. New York: John Day Company, 1947.

Merton, Thomas. *Ishi Means Man.* Greensboro, N.C.: Unicorn Press, 1976.

Miller, Larisa K. "The Secret Treaties with California Indians." *Prologue* magazine (Fall-Winter, 2013). https://www.archives.gov/files/publications/prologue/2013/fall-winter/treaties.pdf.

Mithen, Seven. *After the Ice: A Global Human History 20,000-5000 BC.* UK: Weidenfeld & Nicolson, 2003.

Mooney, James. *The Ghost Dance Religion and the Sioux Outbreak of 1890.* Chicago: University of Chicago Press, 1965.

Myers, Ched and Bob Aldridge. *Resisting the Serpent: Palau's Struggle for Self-Determination.* Baltimore: Fortkamp, 1990.

———. *Watershed Discipleship: Reinhabiting Bioregional Faith and Practice.* Ched Myers, ed. Eugene, OR: Cascade Books, 2016.

———. *Who Will Roll Away the Stone? Discipleship Queries for First World Christians.* Maryknoll, NY: Orbis, 1994.

Mono Lake Committee. "Kutzadika'a People: Living in Harmony with Mono Lake." P.O. Box 29 Lee Vining, CA 93541. http://www.monolake.org/naturalhistory/kutzadikaa.htm.

———. "The Natural History of Mono Lake." P.O. Box 29 Lee Vining, CA 93541. http://www.monolake.org/naturalhistory/stats.htm#Age.

Mumford, Lewis. *The City in History: Its Origins, Its Transformations, and Its Prospects.* New York: Harcourt, Brace and World, 1961.

Neruda, Pablo. *The Heights of Macchu Picchu.* Translated by Nathaniel Tarm. New York: Farrar, Straus and Giroux, 1968.

Neruda, Pablo. Nobel Lecture "Towards the Splendid City." Delivered Dec. 13, 1971. Permission from (c) The Nobel Foundation.

Ong, Walter J. *Orality and Literacy: The Technologizing of the Word.* New York: Methuen, 1982.

Pauketat, Timothy R., and Susan M. Alt. "Medieval Life in America's Heartland." In *Medieval Mississippians: The Cahokian World,* edited by Pauketat and Alt, New Mexico: School for Advanced Research Press, 2015. http://globalmiddleages.org/sites/default/files/MedMiss-01au.pdf

"Remembering the Great Flood of 1993." National Weather Service Forecast Office, St. Louis, MO. https://www.weather.gov/lsx/93flood

Ricketts, Edward F. *Between Pacific Tides*. Stanford, CA: Stanford University Press, 1939.

Roman Catholic Missal. Easter Vigil. "Blessing of Baptismal Water." Section 46. http://www.liturgies.net/Liturgies/Catholic/roman_missal/eastervigillatin.htm

Roman Catholic Catechism. Part Two, Section Two, Chapter 1, Article 1, No. 1213. http://www.vatican.va/archive/ENG0015/__P3G.HTM

Ross, Woodburn O. "John Steinbeck: Naturalism's Priest." *College English* (10, No. 8, 1949). DOI:10.2307/372552.

Samatar, Sofia. *Tender: Stories*. Easthampton, MA: Small Beer Press, 2017.

Seppa, Nathan. "Metropolitan Life on the Mississippi." *The Washington Post*, March 12, 1997. https://www.washingtonpost.com/wp-srv/national/daily/march/12/cahokia.html

Sonoquie, Monique. *The Beginning of the Chumash: A Chumash Oral History*. Chico, CA: Indigenous Youth Foundation, 2003.

Steinbeck, John. *The Log from the Sea of Cortez*. New York: Penguin, 1951.

Stevens, Wallace. "Adagia." In *Opus Posthumous*. New York: Alfred A. Knopf, 1957.

Tu Fu. "Enjoying Rain on a Spring Night." Translated by David Lunde. *Literary Review*. (Vol. 39, Issue 4. NJ: Fairleigh Dickinson University, 1996).

Whitman, Walt. "Passage to India." In *Railroads, Reconstruction, and the Gospel of Prosperity: Aid under the Radical Republicans, 1865-1877* by Mark W. Summers. Princeton: Princeton University Press, 1984.

Timbrook, Jan. "Virtuous Herbs: Plants in Chumash Medicine." *Journal of Ethnobiology*, (Winter, 1987).

Hero, Hawk, and Open Hand: American Indian Art of the Ancient Midwest and South, Richard F. Townsend, general editor. Chicago: The Art Institute of Chicago, Yale University Press, 2004.

Mark Twain In Eruption: Hitherto Unpublished Pages About Men and Events. New York: Harper and Brothers, 1940.

Twain, Mark. *Roughing It*. San Francisco: American Publishing Company, 1872. http://www.classicreader.com/booktoc.php/sid.2/bookid.1407), https://www.gutenberg.org/files/3177/3177-h/3177-h.htm

Walker, Frank X. *Buffalo Dance: The Journey of York*. University Press of Kentucky, 2004.

Winegarner, Beth. "The First Ones: Pomo Lifeways." *Sacred Sonoma*. Lulu.com, 2007. http://www.sacredsonoma.com

Made in the USA
Monee, IL
22 May 2020